My Life With Black Bears

Stories and Photographs of Adventures with my Bear Friends

by Gabriel Mapel, Age 16

www.wildwithgabriel.com

Published by:
Wild Earth
PO Box 18
New Hope, VA 24469
800-871-5647
email: info@wildwithgabriel.com

www.wildwithgabriel.com

Table of Contents

Dedication

For the mama bear and three cubs that were the first bears I ever met on July 6, 2008.
Thank you for changing my life and becoming my very first bear friends.

Acknowledgments

I would like to thank all the bears for the amazing experiences over the past eight years that have enabled me to write this book.

I would like to thank my friend Denise Machado, National Park Ranger and fellow bear advocate, for her profound support of my connection with bears. She has opened her home to me and has spent hours and hours of her time bear watching with me and teaching me about bears. *Thank you so much, Denise,* for enabling me to spend so many extra hours with my bear friends! I would also like to thank my friend and Denise's husband, Rick, for all his support graciously welcoming me into his home so Denise and I could go bear watching together!

I would like to thank my friend Larry Brown for being my first wildlife mentor (after my parents) and teaching me a whole lot of what I know about bears. You were and are a true inspiration and I'll always remember those hundreds of hours we spent together when I was a beginning bear watcher and you were teaching me *everything!*

I would like to thank my friend Rodney Cammauf for being the photographer for my first book, "Oh No, Gertrude!". It was an honor to work with you, Rod, and I look forward to more times bear watching together!

I would like to thank my friend and naturalist Chris Day for her continued support of my connection with bears.

Finally, I would like to thank my Mama and Papa for their most amazing support of me and my connection with the bears and for driving me back and forth to their habitat all those times! I love you guys so much and can't wait for many, many more years of bear watching together!

Author's Note

As a Volunteer Interpretive Ranger with the National Park Service, I am often asked if the Parks give names to the individual bears that are most often seen. The National Park Service does not name bears. However, because I observe and get to know so many different bears, I do give them nicknames in order to keep track of them and their offspring as the generations unfold.

While volunteering, I spend a great deal of time educating people that whenever around bears, it is important to give them the respect and space they deserve (at least 50 yards!), and it is never appropriate to approach bears in order to get the "perfect picture"! While many of the photos I present in this book might lead you to think I was quite close when the photos were taken, all the photos were taken with a 600mm telephoto lens while remaining more than the Park-required 50 yards away from the bears.

Introduction

I'm Gabriel Mapel, a 16-year-old homeschooled nature lover who lives in the Appalachian Mountains of Virginia, and some of my best friends in the world are Black Bears! I am so fortunate that over the last eight years I have been able to spend hundreds of hours each year among Black Bears throughout the East Coast and country. I am very privileged to work as a Volunteer Interpretive Ranger with the National Park Service, specializing in educating visitors about bears, and I plan to pursue park rangering as a career. I feel there is no better way to help bears than educating the public about how to act around bears, right in the heart of their habitat!

I have decided to write this book to bring some of the bear magic I have experienced in these past eight years to you! It is my hope that after you read this book you will become one of my fellow ambassadors for bears, working to help keep them safe and protected! They are misunderstood creatures that need our help to spread the truth about them and their behavior.

A chance encounter in July, 2008 changed my life forever. My dad and I were hiking on the Appalachian Trail through Shenandoah National Park and we spotted my first-ever wild bear off to the right of the trail: a majestic, 250 pound Black Bear. It was a truly thrilling and sacred experience that got more thrilling and more sacred as the seconds went on.

The bear was sitting at the base of a tree and just moments after I laid eyes on her I saw two cubs — weighing just 15 pounds and just six months old — shoot up the tree! Then a couple of trees to the left, and slightly closer to us, another cub shot up! Four bears for my first encounter, including three cubs! We watched for several minutes from the park-required 50 yards, but then realized that the reason the cubs went scurrying up the trees was that their mama had signaled to them that we might be a potential threat. To respect the bears' privacy and space, we backed off and headed down the trail. When we were about 100 yards away we could hear the sounds of the claws of the little cubs climbing down the trees!

My dad and I both left in an amazing state, one that I had never experienced and that would change my life forever. Just from that brief, five minute chance encounter, I knew I had a special bond with bears and that they were my friends. That autumn of 2008 my dad and I took many more trips back to the Park, and we discovered an oak grove where bears were feasting heavily on that fall's bountiful nut supply. We took my mom to that oak grove where she met the bears for her first time, and she, too, fell in love with them.

All too quickly the season came and went. Over that winter I missed the bears an amazing amount, and I realized that this was not just a passing summer hobby and that my connection and friendship with the bears was genuine and would be long-lasting. I gave up all my hobbies and parted ways with my stargazing and train-watching friends, to make time for my new furry friends, and I've never looked back. Ever since, my primary focus each year from April to November has been to spend time with my dear bears, while documenting my experiences with photographs, studying their behavior in depth, and helping them the best I can by making the world a healthier and safer place for them. I can't wait to spend the rest of my life continuing this work!

I have had some of the most amazing experiences in the world and have learned an immeasurable amount of behavioral information firsthand. I have also accumulated a tremendous number of photos and stories, a few of which I have decided to share with you, and I hope that this brief introduction to some of my best friends will help YOU realize how magnificent, misunderstood, and genuinely amazing Black Bears are, and that you, too, will come to understand and help them!

For the love of Bears,
Gabriel

How You Can Help Keep Black Bears Safe

Drive the speed limit! Many Black Bears are killed every year by speeding vehicles. Driving fast in Black Bear country is not only a concern for your safety but a concern for the safety of bears and other wildlife!

Do not feed bears or any other wildlife! This is the cardinal rule of behavior in bear country. Even if you see an emaciated bear and think you are "helping it out," it will then associate humans with food and possibly be named a "nuisance bear" by wildlife officers in which case it will have to be relocated or put down. Feeding bears also makes them lose their fear of humans and become easier targets for speeders and poachers.

Do not leave your food unattended in bear country, even for a moment! Countless times each year I walk through a picnic area or campground and come across unattended food on a picnic table. More times than not the owner returns within five minutes. I politely ask them to next time please clean up their food before they leave, even if for just a few minutes to use the bathroom or move their car. A bear could quickly get their food, which is nearly as bad as actually feeding a bear!

Take every scrap of food with you! It is VERY important when recreating in bear country to leave all picnic sites, campsites, and backcountry sites clean — pack up all of your trash and ALL your food scraps and immediately dispose of them in bear-proof dumpsters or trash cans. Countless times each year I walk through picnic areas and campgrounds and find food scraps left under a picnic table or in a fire pit. Generally they are biodegradable — watermelon rinds, corn husks, pieces of fruit, etc. — and I'm sure people think "it will biodegrade, it is not an issue," but it IS an issue in bear country! Be sure to triple-check your site before you leave and take EVERYTHING with you.

Always properly store your food and trash while picnicking and camping! If a bear approaches while picnicking, secure all your food immediately and then scare the bear away. After eating, if there is no bear proof trash can available, or if it is full, take your trash with you! Keep all your food with you or in a *locked* vehicle with the windows rolled ALL THE WAY UP! Black Bears can open unlocked car doors and break windows that are the least bit cracked open! Also, NEVER take food or scented items, such as toothpaste, into your tent!

Never run from a bear! When hiking in the woods I encounter dozens of people each year who ask me if it is okay to run from a bear. NO! NOT AT ALL! Running from a bear could provoke the bear's predator instinct and it may give chase which would result in officials naming the bear "dangerous" and possibly euthanizing it.

Know what to do if you encounter a bear while hiking! The first thing I always remember when hiking in bear country is that I am in their home, not mine. Black Bears are very tolerant of humans and usually happy to share their home, but only if we respect them! Always remain 50 yards away from Black Bears and if you spot one and you are closer than 50 yards, back away slowly. Again, NEVER run! If a bear approaches you, yell and shout, clap your hands and/or throw rocks at the bear to scare it away. In the extremely rare event that the Black Bear makes contact, always FIGHT BACK and do not play dead (like you should with a Grizzly). If you encounter a highly aggressive bear, report it to rangers or wildlife officials as soon as you can.

Follow dog regulations! Bears and dogs do not mix! Always comply with regulations regarding where, when, and how dogs are allowed. NEVER hike in bear country with an unleashed dog!

Understand Black Bear communication! Black Bears are very intelligent animals (in fact they are the most intelligent non-human land mammals in North America) and they communicate with each other and also with us. If you understand bear language you will be able to appropriately react when a bear starts talking to you! :) Bears will most often communicate with you when they are upset with you and want you to leave their territory. "Huffing" (a blowing sound) expresses their first level of agitation and is often followed by the second level of agitation which is "popping jaws" (when bears actively clack their teeth repeatedly). If a bear performs either one of these communications it is recommended that you leave immediately, even if you are more than 50 yards away. Again, back away slowly but do not run! The third level of agitation is a lunge. This occurs when a bear suddenly advances a short distance while huffing or popping its jaws. This may include jumping up on the side of a tree or swatting the ground. Again, leave immediately by backing away slowly. The fourth and rarest level of communication and agitation is a "bluff charge." No matter how hard it may be, DO NOT RUN during a bluff charge. To learn more about bluff charges and my first bluff charge, see the story on page 28.

Know what to do if you encounter a bear along the roadside! Black Bears in the frontcountry of the Appalachian Mountains are often highly habituated to humans and will feed right along the side of the road, which makes for a perfect opportunity for visitors to have a chance to see them! Dozens of times every year I will be driving behind someone who is driving the speed limit, but then once they spot a bear it seems as if safety goes out the window! Many times I have seen people park in the middle of the road, in the opposing lane of traffic, or on a sharp bend and get out and leave their vehicle so they don't miss the bear photo. This not only causes a dangerous situation for humans but it also causes a potentially dangerous situation for bears. Many times I have seen a Black Bear run *right through* a "bear jam" (a traffic jam caused by a bear sighting) and if a vehicle was trying to get around an illegally and dangerously parked vehicle, it could hit the bear! If you encounter a bear along the roadside, keep driving unless you can find a way to pull completely out of the lane of traffic. Then stay in your vehicle to watch the bear and ONLY get out if it is more than 50 yards away from the road and then be sure to stay on the opposite side of the road from the bear.

Stash your trash! If you live in bear country it is recommended that you put your trash out the morning of pickup, not the night before. Black Bears are active at night and a bear could easily get into your trash which could put it in danger. Once it becomes habituated to human food & trash and is labeled a "problem bear," wildlife officials will have to remove or euthanize it.

Spread the word about bears! I have written this book to educate people about bears. I hope that after reading this book that every reader will understand that bears are generally docile, timid and extremely misunderstood animals. The more that we as bear advocates spread the word and make people realize that they are not the dangerous monsters that the media makes them out to be, the more people will join us in helping to protect them.

Thank you for your help!

The First Days of Spring

Black Bears emerge from their winter dens from late March to early April after their long winter of rest. Each year when spring comes around I head out to the forest to scour every place where I've previously seen a bear, in hopes of finding my first bear of the year. One April a friend of mine found the first bear of the year before I did. He was kind enough to tell me where it was and he met my dad and me there the following day to look for her.

It was a large adult female, all by herself, but we could tell that she was a mama bear that still had cubs in the den as we could see her lactating nipples. Cubs are born to their mother's breasts in their winter den in January or February, and they are with her constantly until April when they emerge from the den into the outer world. Once mama bear brings her cubs out of the den, they will only rarely be so close to each other, when she nurses them. The rest of the time they will be spread out, walking through the woods, in sight of each other, but with much less physical contact.

To prepare the cubs for their emergence into the wide world, what does mama bear do? She leaves the den for periods of several hours without the cubs to teach them how to be independent of her before she brings them out into the world. That is exactly what my dad, our friend, and I witnessed on that particular day!

She was extremely lethargic and spent most of her time sleeping at the base of an oak tree. She foraged on the early leaf shoots of spring for an hour or so, but the majority of the six hours were spent sleeping.

As the day drew to a close she climbed up the special tree under which she had spent most of her time sleeping. There was a large hole leading into a hollow part of the tree, and we wondered if that was the den that held her cubs. But when she climbed up the tree, she went to sleep on a branch right next to the hole! Finally, after nearly another hour of rest, she went into the hole.

What happened next was something that I'll never, ever forget. As we walked back to the trailhead, along the trail that happened to pass right under the den tree, we heard the most amazing sounds: purring and cooing noises coming from inside the tree! We listened for several minutes in complete awe. What we were hearing was the sound of the cubs nursing and expressing their joy that their mama was back home again! That sound of nursing cubs in their den was one of the most incredible sounds I've ever heard in nature and the perfect way to end an awesome day!

The Den Tree: Arrow points to the den opening!
Black Bears often den in hollow trees. 9

Climbing School

It was a sunny, cold, and windy late April afternoon and I was hiking through one of my favorite places on Earth when I looked off to my left and found an adult female bear that I know well at the base of a large White Pine tree. It was great to see her again as I hadn't seen her since the previous October. I was also excited knowing she probably had cubbies hiding somewhere as it had been two years since her last litter, and female Black Bears give birth every other year.

After watching her through binoculars from quite a distance I eventually found her treasures: two little babies that had been nestled beneath her the entire time I'd been watching her, hiding out of view of the outside world!

As I continued to watch this gorgeous family, mama bear got up from lying down and snuggling her little ones, and she encouraged her cubs to climb the White Pine. The cubs climbed up four or five feet, and then one climbed down safely and the other fell down! Mama gently urged them to keep practicing and they both got up to about ten feet before climbing back down. I soon realized that what I was watching was the mama bear building the cubs' confidence levels and teaching them that it is safe to climb high up trees — as they would need to be expert climbers for the rest of their lives! Although cubs are able to climb as soon as they emerge from their dens, it is important for mama bears to slowly build their confidence levels so that they can quickly climb a tree if a threat arrives in the area. Eventually they made it up to about forty feet, where they nestled in a notch of the tree, and fell asleep.

After a several hour nap they climbed back down and mama led them deeper into the woods, out of my view. I decided to walk over to the tree to see where the cubs had spent so much time climbing and sleeping. At the base of the pine tree I noticed that mama bear had made a bed of sticks, grass, and pine needles. This bed was useful both as a comfortable place for mama and the cubs to lie during their time at the tree and it also served to cushion the cubs' falls, as one of the cubs did while I was watching!

As I continued to explore the woods, fifty yards away I found another pine tree, this one with bigger grooves in the bark making it easier to climb, and a nicer bed at the base made of leaves and pine needles. It was even hollowed out a little bit, and certainly softer than the first bed. Eventually all the pieces of the puzzle were coming together. I realized that before I found the mama and cubs she had first taken them to this easier-to-climb tree with a much softer bed at the base to cushion their falls. And then, once the cubs mastered this introductory climbing tree, she took them to the more difficult tree to climb, where I saw them practicing. I assume that she continued to work up to more and more difficult-to-climb trees until the cubs fully mastered climbing so that they could climb any tree at any time with no bed at the base!

It was such an awesome experience to be able to witness these cubs in the first few days out of the den and while they were still building their confidence levels as climbers!

One of the Climbing School trees, with soft bed at base

11

The Multi-Day Cub Fest

I took these photos while experiencing a multi-day cub-fest, one of the most unique and amazing experiences I have ever had with Black Bears!

My friend and I were birdwatching in the mountains one mid-April day and one of the places we stopped was where the two of us had seen a mama bear and her single cub the previous spring. They had been up high in an oak tree very soon after emerging from their den.

While my friend and I were bird watching, I spotted a black object at the base of that same tree and alerted my friend, "I think I've got a bear!"

We looked through our binoculars and my theory was confirmed! I had found the same mama bear, this time all by herself. We left delighted, and given that it was only mid-April, I assumed that the single cub that we had seen the previous spring — which would now be a yearling — was still sleeping in their den somewhere nearby.

My mom and I returned later that day, and got a surprise! A bittersweet surprise. The sweetness was that there were three, tiny, 4-8 pound cubs climbing on the tree, just newly emerged from their winter den! They were some of the youngest cubs I had ever seen and it was a truly amazing experience to see them! But the bitterness was that the mama bear had new cubs and the cub from the previous spring was gone!

Female bears generally mate and have cubs every other year, booting their offspring on their own when they are a year and a half old. My suspicion is that the cub from the previous spring had died sometime before the June-July mating season, which allowed the mama to go into estrus and mate a year early so that she could have these new cubs.

I was able to return to this spot at least once a day, and on days two through five the bears were all there — mama and her 3 precious babies. And then on day 6 they were gone! I suspect that after five days of eating catkins (spring shoots of oak & ash trees) in this tree near their den they were then ready to head out for the year of exploring throughout their territory.

It was an absolutely incredible experience that I feel so honored to have witnessed. To be able to watch the cubs and their mama each and every day for nearly a week was so unusual and special. I returned the following spring and the mama and all three of her offspring, then yearlings, were there in the same tree again! She may have lost her first cub, but she more than made up for it by successfully raising three the following year!

Meeting the Next Generation (Year 1)

One late April day my dad and I found a mama bear and her three young cubs deep in the woods. We instantly recognized her as a mama that we had spent a lot of time with two years earlier, when she was raising three different cubs. It was so wonderful to see her again and learn that she had given birth to her second straight litter of triplets!

When we first found this gorgeous new family, the three cubs were sleeping up high in a large tree while mama guarded the base and foraged on young plant material on the forest floor.

After the cubs had a long rest up in the tree, mama bear made a soft grunting noise indicating that she wanted them to climb down the tree. Two of the cubs came down right away, but the third took a few minutes longer. It was so sweet to see mama go to the base of the tree and greet each cub nose-to-nose as they reached her.

It was a wonderful, first-of-many encounters with this special bear family, and I am so grateful that I got to see them so soon after emerging from their birth den.

Meeting the Next Generation (Year 2)

After spending a lot of time with this special bear family during their first year, the story continued the following spring! The encounter during which I took this photograph took place on April 17th, just a couple of weeks earlier than the date on which I had first met that family the previous spring.

Spring is always one of the most exciting times in the forest, and I get much joy and happiness visiting my bear friends after not seeing them for many months. It's always a wonderful sight when familiar faces show up after making it through the winter. Occasionally a bear I love will not show up in the spring, and I have to come to the sad conclusion that it didn't make it through the winter. When this happens, it is often a cub from a large family that doesn't make it through its first winter.

After spending so much time with this family while the youngsters were cubs of the year, I hoped that all three would make it through their first full winter. I felt pretty confident because the last time I saw them, before they entered their winter den, the cubs were large and looked very healthy.

When I took this photo my dad and I were hiking in the heart of this family's habitat with the specific hope of finding this family to see how they were faring after the winter. As we approached our turnaround point for the hike, we heard some commotion up ahead. And then, as we walked farther up the trail, we found the source of the commotion. It was our mama bear friend and all 3 of her yearlings! It was a huge relief to know that all 4 of them had made it through the winter, and there was nothing more special then getting to spend some more quality time with some very good friends of mine after not seeing them for five months!

Bear Salad

One early May evening my dad and I were out looking for bears and we came across this handsome fellow: a large, powerful, adult male bear. We ended up spending several hours with him that evening, as unlike most adult male bears he was not at all bothered by our presence. The reason? He had been out of his winter den for only a few weeks and was focused on regaining the third of his body weight that he had lost during the winter! He was feasting on low-growth forest-floor vegetation, the young grasses and flowers that cover the forest floor during early spring. I prefer to call it "Bear Salad"!

As the evening drew to a close and nightfall took over the forest, my dad and I headed back to our campsite, so happy about the evening that we had just spent with this bear. We returned the next morning, mainly just to relive our experience of the day before, but we got a welcome surprise when we arrived back at the "Salad Bar".

Lo and behold, there he was, continuing to feast on "Bear Salad"! I wondered if he'd stayed there and eaten all night or if he'd left and returned. I continued to come back to this spot and for the next three weeks this bear was almost always there whenever I looked for him. He had a nearly unlimited supply of "Bear Salad" and was dominant enough that he could keep it all to himself without other bears challenging him for it!

The last time I saw him there was on May 26th and he was acting differently. He was moving faster, eating less, and seemed to be on a mission. All for a good reason, too, as the June and July Black Bear mating season was just around the corner. As one of the dominant males of the Black Bear community, his job was now to go become a papa. He would have two months to mate with females and spread his genes to make sure that his genetic line would thrive and succeed. I was sad that my time with this big boy at the "Salad Bar" was coming to an end but I had hopes that maybe I could catch up with him during the mating season, when he would be acting very differently, with his game face on.

The Tale of Little Monster

This is a yearling bear that I first met one May afternoon when he was a young cub on a walkabout with his mom and two siblings through the woods.

I had the opportunity over the course of that year to study this cooperative bear family's behavior first-hand, and I quickly noticed that the behavior of each of the three cubs was unique. One of them was quite like its mama: mellow, sweet, and innocent, with not a care in the world. Another cub had a similar personality, but with the additional, very interesting personality trait of being EXTREMELY independent and adventurous! This cub would always wander and follow 50-75 yards behind its mama and two siblings! She was one of the most adventurous cubs that I've ever met, truly an eccentric but sweet little bear who has now grown into a beautiful, young adult female.

And then there's this one, the third cub of the litter who I nicknamed "Little Monster". When you get to know a 3-litter, there is often one cub that is just a little bit eccentric. And I guess the "adventurous cub" wasn't enough eccentricity for this litter, because Little Monster was even more eccentric!

Little Monster always seemed uneasy. There was always something wrong. After all, the world was out to get him, right? Well, evidently that's what he thought!

Huffing and jaw popping are defensive acts generally performed by males in mating season or by mothers with young cubs that are uneasy around humans or other potential threats in their vicinity. One thing is for sure: cubs are generally not the bears that huff and jaw pop. Unless you are Little Monster!

Generally, when I was in the presence of Little Monster's family, his mom and two siblings would be comfortable with me. But Little Monster was not! He would huff and jaw pop at me, even if I was 75 yards away! It was the most hilarious thing in the world to watch a young cub, just 6 months old, acting so "aggressively."

I could only imagine that he was a young male and one day would turn into a feisty mating season warrior, just like a large male in his territory that I know well and that may well be Little Monster's dad.

One day while watching this family in the second May that Little Monster was alive, three of the family were foraging, while Little Monster was taking a nap behind a tree. I was able to walk farther up the trail and watch Little Monster from about 50 yards away, as he took his nap. It was the first time I had ever been in Little Monster's presence without huffing and jaw popping. Once he woke up, he gave me a quick, gentle stare, and then in his typical fashion, he jumped up onto the side of the tree with jaws popping, even though I was 50 yards away from him and even farther away from the rest of his family!

After his mama sent her three yearlings, including Little Monster, out on their own in June, I was a little sad that my time with Little Monster as a cub was coming to an end. And I wondered how he'd act on his own. Well, I quickly found out. He hid! I've only seen him a few times since he's been on his own, and he always ran at the first sight of me! He's definitely an eccentric little bear that I feel honored to have met and know.

Gertrude

This is a very special bear, an amazing mama bear, that is very near and dear to my heart. I call her Gertrude. I first met Gertrude back in 2009 when she was three years old and was raising an unusually large first litter of three cubs. Some naughty picnickers left their food out on a picnic table while they went for a hike and Gertrude ate it. As a result she became "food conditioned" and had to be removed from her home territory because she became a picnic area "nuisance." Gertrude was relocated 70 miles south where she had to fight for or struggle to find new territory. Simply put, her life was put at risk because people did not clean up their food! I loved Gertrude so much and was so saddened by the situation she was put in that I decided to write a book about her to teach other people about how to act in bear country. Accompanied by the stunning photographs taken by my friend and professional photographer, Rodney Cammauf, we pulled off a book that has been amazingly successful in educating people about how to behave around bears and keep them safe! (More information about this book, titled "Oh No, Gertrude!", can be found at the end of this book.)

I was concerned that I'd never see my friend Gertrude again after she was moved to a remote area, and a bear's survival chances are not all that high when it is relocated. During that fall of 2009 I was lucky enough to actually see her once in her new home. I looked for her again in 2010, with no success. And then in 2011, I was given one of the most welcome surprises that I've ever received. Through the grapevine I received word that Gertrude had been sighted back in her original territory — she had walked 70 miles and found her way back home!

When I went to that area to see for myself, I was actually quite surprised to find that, unlike in 2009, Gertrude was hard to find. After many trips and hours, my mom and I finally located Gertrude with three new cubs one day in late June. We spent about half an hour with her and got to marvel at the beauty of her and her young ones. We could tell it was Gertrude because when she was relocated park rangers had applied a yellow ear tag to her left ear so that she would be identifiable if she was ever sighted again. She had beaten the odds. She had lived. And she was home!

That amazing encounter, one that I'll never forget, was my only time with my dear friend Gertrude in 2011. I heard reports of her being sighted alone in 2012, after she booted her yearlings, but I never saw her that year. In late May, 2013 I located her in the heart of her territory with three more cubs! Three litters into her mothering life and she was raising her seventh, eighth, and ninth cubs! That's what I call an amazing, productive mama!

I only saw Gertrude twice in 2013 and then several times in 2014 after she booted all three of her third litter. In 2015 she gave birth to her fourth litter, this time of two cubs (a small litter for her) but they were two of the sweetest and healthiest cubs I've ever known, and you could tell that they were Gertrude's children by their personalities and health alone. Whenever I see Gertrude it is an amazing experience as she is such a survivor. She is a unique, proven bear, and one of my very best bear friends. And I am ever so grateful that she has not gotten into trouble again since 2009, and I hope that she can live a full life in her true home! I still find it jaw-dropping that she walked 70 miles to get back home. Gertrude is a truly determined bear: she beat the odds, walked such a long way back home, stayed out of trouble, and always successfully raises her cubs.

She Learned Her Lesson... A few years after Gertrude walked back home I was watching her in the very picnic area where she first got in trouble. She walked up to a picnic table where a picnicker had not cleaned up some pork barbecue, sniffed it, and left it alone. That was the ultimate proof to me that Gertrude learned her lesson and will not get back in trouble ever again!

Gertrude after she returned home.
Notice her yellow ear tag.

The Story of Sky

I have had the amazing privilege of being able to watch many of my bear friends grow and develop over a number of years. However, this bear that I call Sky is unique. She is a bear that I have watched struggle through hard times only to rise to be an amazing mama once again. I have had many wonderful encounters with her and want to share with you the multi-year story of my relationship with Sky.

I first met Sky one June day when she was raising three cubs. Sky was a skittish mama that would run when she first spotted humans. One time she hung around just long enough for me to capture a good facial photo that I could use to help me recognize her in the future.

The next time I met up with Sky was the following June, about a year after I first met her. As expected, she had already sent her yearlings out on their own. But what surprised me was now that she wasn't caring for cubs, she was a much mellower bear, and my mom and I got to spend some quality time with her without her running off. One day she even caught a White-tailed Deer fawn and ate it 50 yards away from us! It was the first time I ever saw a bear catch a fawn, which I have since witnessed several times — a sad and yet amazing part of the natural circle of life in the wild.

When I next met up with her a few weeks later, my heart sank. She was limping quite badly with an injured rear leg. I wondered if she had been hit by a car or maybe had gotten into a fight with a male during mating season. I only hoped that my friend Sky would persevere and get through this tough situation.

I did not see Sky again for several months, but in October I found her and I was so relieved that she was still alive! She was still limping, but not as badly, and it seemed like her condition had improved. The encounter was brief but I was so hopeful that she would make it through the winter.

In May the following year my hope became reality. She showed up in her usual haunts! It was so wonderful to find Sky alive. She did pay a small price for her injury the previous year, however. Female Black Bears have cubs every other year, and Sky was "scheduled" to have cubs that year (the year after her injury), and she showed up cub-less. I had been unsure if she would have had a chance to mate before her injury, but evidently she hadn't. As excited as I had been to see little baby Skies, this was a small price to pay. She was alive!

In June of that year I had one of the most incredible encounters I ever have had with Sky. My mom and I located her being courted by a large male, and they proceeded to mate within our view! It was the first time I had ever witnessed Black Bears mating and it felt so special that the once-injured Sky was a part of it. And now I was ever so hopeful that Sky would have cubs the following year.

By the time the following year came around I was anxiously awaiting Sky sightings — very anxiously awaiting them because I was concerned that her injuries may have affected her ability to give birth. When June came and went and I hadn't spotted her in her usual hangouts, I was concerned. I finally found a photo online of a sow that looked like Sky with two new cubs. I contacted the photographer to confirm the location, and when he said it was in the heart of Sky's territory, I was so relieved that she was okay and that the mating that I had seen the previous year had been successful! About two weeks later my mom and I met up with Sky, our only time with her that year, and it was so amazing to spend time watching the cubs that we had witnessed being conceived the previous year.

I saw Sky several times the following year, first with her yearlings before she sent them on their own, and then later in the mating season. Last year Sky raised another litter of two cubs. I have a feeling Sky is a fairly old bear and I don't know how many more times she will have cubs, but I feel really honored to have been able to spend a lot of time with her over the course of three litters and she has treated me to some of the most incredible experiences I've ever had with bears.

The Boot

One May afternoon my mom and I were in the heart of the territory of an adult female bear that we know well. The previous year she had given birth to three cubs and we knew that within a month she would be kicking them out, or "booting" them as I call it. A mama Black Bear keeps her offspring for about 16 months and then sends them on their own so that she can mate again and have her next litters of cubs, 24 months after her previous litter.

We were lucky enough to find our beautiful bear friend and were looking around for her yearlings. It was the third week of May, just at the onset of the time of year when mamas generally boot their yearlings, and I didn't expect that this mama would have "booted" just yet. However, much to our surprise, as we looked around we did not see her yearlings anywhere! We came to the conclusion that she had very recently booted them. We spent about 30 minutes watching the female bear and then continued up the road.

Less than a mile away we came across another bear, the one pictured above. As we watched this beautiful bear, I noticed how small it was. A good facial view clinched it for me: I recognized that face — this was one of the yearling offspring of the adult female that we had just seen! As the minutes passed by, another similarly sized bear walked out onto the road about 60 yards in front of us. A quick view of her face confirmed it as one of the three yearlings! Then, as if that 1-2 punch wasn't enough, the third yearling walked out onto the road behind us!

The explanation for such an interesting encounter with three yearlings was clear: mama bear had very recently booted them and they were still hanging out near each other. This is fairly typical behavior of yearlings soon after the boot.

After spending some time with the three dazed and confused little ones separated from their mother for the first time in their lives, I headed home. I had watched these cubs with their mama since the previous spring when they were quite young, and she had done everything to help make sure that they would be able to thrive without her. She had successfully raised all three cubs to the point in life when they were now able to start surviving on their own and that overjoyed me!

Summertime Love, err Drama!

June and July are Black Bear mating season and it is always one of my favorite times of year in the woods. Mating season is a thrilling experience for bear watchers like myself. Massive adult males like the large, tested warrior pictured here are generally extremely secretive; for most of the year they rarely come into view. The one exception to this unwritten rule? Mating Season!

It is a truly wonderful experience to get to observe these huge, dominant, moody bears doing what they do best: defending their territory, courting their sows and spreading their genes around the bear world!

It is also an interesting time of year to observe adult female bears. Females have cubs every other year, so in a given year roughly half of the adult females will be mating. Black Bear mating season is not exactly romantic and females will often refuse to accept males, but the males will not give up easily. It is quite exhilarating to see a large male quickly following a female bear around the woods waiting for her to let him know she is ready to mate!

Males will fight each other for dominance over territory or for mating rights of a specific female. If you look closely at this photo, you will see that this big guy has a couple of battle scars on his face. Just a week earlier he did not have these scars, so I suspect they resulted from a fight with another large male in his territory. Most of the time males only sustain minor injuries like these from fighting, but occasionally injuries are more damaging and it will take time for the bear to recover. Fights are very rarely fatal, though they are not unheard of.

Simply put, June and July are some of the most important months in the bear world and set the stage for the next generation to be born. I love spending time in the woods during these months and getting my chance to witness the drama first-hand.

Witnessing Courtship and Conception

One June day my mom and I were out looking for bears in one of our favorite places where there is a high concentration of Black Bears. We found an adult female that we know well and she was being followed by a nearly 350 pound, handsome adult male. They were about 50 yards off the road and we pulled over, sat down on a stone wall, and ended up watching them for nearly two hours! During that time the male would repeatedly attempt to mount the female, but she was not yet ready for that. Whenever he tried to mount her, she would stand up on her back legs, swat at him, and make some very unique clacking vocalizations.

Several times they actually danced around on their hind legs and wrestled for 5-10 seconds at a time. It was just stunning to witness first-hand. The best way to describe it would be as a flirtatious wrestling match between two bears!

The female would then move a short distance, with the male following. Whenever he tried to mount her again, she repeated the previous behavior of standing up on her hind legs, swatting at him, and vocalizing. This dance went on for about an hour and a half. Sometimes she would run full speed with him right behind her. Twice they sat down next to each other and licked each others' faces. This was a pair that had just gotten together and this was their courtship ritual.

Sometimes female bears will not accept males and will attempt to chase them off. Before a female bear chooses to accept a male and let him mate with her, they do this courtship ritual. Through my many years of bear watching I had seen pairs in the actual act of mating a very few times, and countless times I had seen a female being followed by a male that she had accepted, but I had never, ever seen this courtship ritual first hand. It was an eye-opening, jaw-dropping and incredibly rare event to witness with my own eyes.

The following evening, some 30 hours later, we refound the pair about a half mile away from where we had witnessed the courtship ritual the previous day, and to our amazement the male was actually on top of the female. The female had finally accepted the male and they were in the act of mating!

It was one of the most amazing two days of my bear watching "career" to be able to witness a ~350 pound male and ~150 pound female join up with each other, dance the courtship ritual, and then later see that the female had accepted the male and see the pair mate successfully.

The following year my parents and I were able to find this same adult female bear with her two new cubs. It was such a special thing to be able to spend time with these cubs, knowing that we had witnessed one of them being conceived!

The Bluff Charge

It was an early July afternoon, about five years after first encountering bears, when I had an experience that I will never, ever forget.

Through my first five years of bear watching I had countless experiences that opened my eyes to the fact that Black Bears are almost always gentle, docile, and misunderstood beings. I almost always feel completely safe around bears but a couple of times each year I do get nervous around them. However, it always turns out that the bear does not mean me harm, and more times than not what is concerning me is something going on between two bears and not about me at all.

This particular experience *was* about me, and although it turned out to not be dangerous in any way, it was an eye-opening experience that got my heart going quite possibly faster than it had ever gone before!

I was hiking along one of my favorite trails when I spotted a large, dominant, 400-pound adult male bear about 75 yards ahead of me and off to the left of the trail. He was foraging on forest-floor vegetation, looked up at me, and continued foraging. The saying goes that everyone makes mistakes, and perhaps I made one that day, though I am not really sure. I felt that there would be no harm remaining roughly 75 yards away from the bear and watching the handsome big guy from there. A lot of national parks, including the one I was in, have a rule that you must stay 50 yards away from bears, and I was definitely more than 50 yards from this guy.

One Black Bear myth is that mothers with cubs are the most potentially dangerous bears. *Yes*, mama bears will do anything to protect their cubs and it is always important to respect them and give them their space, but males in mating season are the bears that I am most cautious around as they will naturally, and occasionally aggressively, defend their territory or potential partner.

And on this particular day 75 yards *was not enough* for this big guy intent on protecting his territory! After a couple of minutes of foraging in my presence, he looked up, huffed, snapped a branch with his front paws and then started running at me at full speed. Full speed for a Black Bear is about 30 mph so imagine a 400 pound, potentially dangerous animal running right towards you at 30 mph and you can begin to understand how I felt that day!

My body was telling me my life was coming to an end and all my instincts said to "RUN!" But my head knew this was a "bluff charge" — something I'd heard and read about for five years but never experienced. A bluff charge is a bear's most blatant way of saying "GET OUT OF MY TERRITORY NOW!" — a natural but nerve wracking communication. Knowing this, I did what I highly recommend anyone else also do if ever in the same situation: *I just stood there*, with my arms up making myself look big, and spoke with a loud but calm voice, "Whoa Bear!" "Good Bear!" "You're OK Bear!" This communicated to the bear that I was standing my ground and not backing off, as that — or even more problematically, running away — would invite the bear to possibly follow or give chase. Once the bear got to within 10 yards of me, he did what I knew he would do: he suddenly stopped, turned around and ambled off in the other direction. He successfully delivered his message loud and clear that he needed me out of his territory! As soon as Mr. Bear turned around and started moving off in the other direction, I turned around and headed back to the trailhead. I could save this trail for another day — for now it belonged to Mr. Bear and only Mr. Bear!

Did You Know? Unprovoked Black Bear attacks on humans are extremely rare and most are not fatal. Black Bears are large, powerful and potentially dangerous creatures that need to be treated with great respect but they are misunderstood and not human-killing, dangerous beasts as they are often portrayed.

A Stormy Day of Cherries

One June day I was hiking through the woods and came across this gorgeous, adult female bear. She soon climbed up what I instantly recognized as a cherry tree. Different species of cherry tree fruit at different times of year. This particular cherry tree was fruiting and Mrs. Bear had plans of taking full advantage! Full advantage to the point of not even caring about a THUNDERSTORM!

As I watched her up in her cherry tree, she ate the perfectly ripe, red cherries for about 20 minutes and then a strong and very intense thunderstorm hit. I normally would have headed for cover but I was very curious to see what Mrs. Bear would do, so I huddled under the canopy of a big tree and waited out the storm, keeping my eye on this bear way up in the cherry tree.

I expected she would either climb down to take cover or perhaps settle in on a branch a little lower down in the tree. To my surprise she just stayed there, near the top of the tree, and ate her cherries throughout the entire storm! It was a really neat lesson about how bears are not fazed by such a formidable force of nature!

Berry Bears

One July day my friend and I came across this two year old bear in a large Blackberry patch. July is sometimes a month of hardship for the bear community because food becomes scarcer. Most cherry trees fruit in either June or August and the "Bear Salad" from spring has become inedible mature grasses and flowers. Blackberries, Black Raspberries, Wineberries and a host of other berries are instrumental to Black Bear health in mid-summer and become the biggest part of their diet during this sometimes hard time of year.

This "teenage" bear ate quite a lot from this berry patch that particular July and I thoroughly enjoyed the chance to spend a lot of time with him in his habitat.

Two year old bears like this one crack me up every time I see them because of their big Mickey Mouse-like ears and long, lanky legs! It's like they just haven't grown into some parts of their body yet, and two year olds are arguably the funniest bears in terms of physical appearance. So next time you are out in the woods and think you may be seeing a two year old bear, you don't even need to ask for its birth certificate, you can just check out its ears and legs and you will have your answer!

Picnic Table Bears

Negative human-bear interactions are one of the leading threats to Black Bears. Some of the most problematic human-bear interactions are those that take place in picnic areas and campgrounds. This is a case in point: a small, adult female Black Bear whose life was nearly put at risk because of careless people.

This pretty lady and her three cubs were frequenting a national park campground one July because the Blackberry and Raspberry crop in that campground was very plentiful, and she and other bears were there to take full advantage of it! The park is their home, not ours, and it is our job to make sure to keep a bear-friendly camp if we are going to stay in the middle of their berry patch! Fortunately, most people were doing just that and this bear family got to enjoy their berries for several weeks while we humans had the honor of getting to watch them during our camping trips. Despite hanging out at the campground berry patch, Mrs. Bear would always be a little skittish and would often run away at the sight of me, just like a normal, wild bear.

One day I located her and noticed she was acting differently. With her cubs following, she would walk right by cars, through the campsites, and even the sounds of generators would not faze her. I suspected that someone had fed her, which is the number one NO-NO when it comes to ethical bear watching and a huge violation of park rules.

In mid-July she started approaching people while they were eating, sometimes at their picnic tables, sometimes by their car, sometimes while snacking on a hike. During the morning of the last day of July, her bad behavior peaked. I was standing along the campground loop road, and this now well-known campground bear and her cubs started to enter a campsite. The campers were inside their trailer, unaware that a bear was walking into their camp. I alerted them, "You know you guys have a bear and her cubs coming in!" They said "Thank you, my toast is on the picnic table, I'll go get it!" They quickly pulled their toast into their camper. When the mama bear approached the picnic table without any food on it and put her paws on the table, I assumed it would be fine for her to climb onto the table if she decided to.

When she did climb up onto the picnic table, the camper told me "My medicine is on there, is it bad if she gets that?" The answer was certainly "*Yes!*" It's bad enough for a bear to get hold of anything with a human scent on it, but especially medicine! Who knows what that could do to her body. Fortunately, I was able to yell at Mrs. Bear, clap my hands, and scare her off, just seconds before she was going to consume the medicine.

As a habituated bear who was approaching people and wanting their food, the Park Service set a live trap for her and her cubs' relocation. This would put their lives at risk (because after her relocation she would have to fight for new territory and possibly not get the nourishment she would need to survive). Fortunately, just before they set the trap, the wild food source in the area changed, and she and her cubs stopped coming into the campground and were never relocated. I felt fortunate to be a small part of an intense few weeks for this special bear family and a small part of helping to save them.

Sociable Cubbies

One day my mom and I found a mama bear and her two cubs along the side of a mountain road and had the honor of spending time with them.

They were foraging in a roadside berry patch for about 20 minutes. Then they wandered off into the woods and as we headed back to our car we heard something in the bushes behind us.

A cute little cub, one of the two, was curious and came out of the bushes to have another look at us! He just sat there looking at us for about 30 seconds before running back into the woods to meet up with mama and sibling. It was just such an adorable, wonderful end to a fantastic encounter.

A couple months later, once they had grown quite a bit, I re-found the family. Mama Bear quickly led them away from my parents and me. Once again the cubs became curious and climbed up on a log to check us out. It was so cute and reminded me so much of my first time seeing them.

Searching for Protein

Eastern Black Bears have a protein-deficient diet for much of the year. Eighty percent of their diet is composed of vegetarian matter and the other 20% does not come easily! Black Bears do not like to work hard for their food, but a certain times of year they do have to put in extra effort to find enough protein.

For protein, Black Bears delight in coming across road-killed or naturally-killed mammals that they can feast on, and in the spring they take full advantage of an occasional young, easy-to-hunt White-tailed Deer fawn.

However, their most consistent source of protein all season long comes from larvae: ant larvae, bee larvae, and grubs! It is very common when watching bears in the Appalachian woods, especially in the middle of summer, to see a bear lifting up a rock to look for larvae underneath. They lift up the rock with their paw, stick their head in, and eat what they find!

Did you know? Most people believe that Black Bears raid beehives for their honey. Although they do enjoy honey, the main reason they attack beehives and put up with bee stings is to eat the bee larvae, a much-needed source of protein!

A Peek Into the Life of Subadult Bears

One August evening I was fortunate enough to find and have an amazing encounter with this beautiful bear family. My dad and I were driving on a forest road, and at the edge of the road we spotted a family of bears. Given that mama bears generally send their yearlings on their own between late May and late June, I obviously assumed that the family would be a mama and her cubs of the year. But when I got a good look at them, I realized that the two cubs were far too big to be cubs of the year — their bodies and especially faces were way too large and developed to be that young.

We were looking at a mama Black Bear and two yearlings, in August! I was puzzled. Why did she still have them with her, two months after she should have sent them on their own? We spent about 15 minutes observing this very interesting bear family before they retreated deep into the woods.

I have since learned that subadult female Black Bears will occasionally rejoin their mama bear post-mating season. The main reason that the mama bears boot their yearlings in late May and early June is so that they can mate again in June-July. If her daughters re-find their mama once mating season has passed, it is not uncommon for mama to let them travel with her for a period of days, weeks, or even months. Female Black Bears will not allow their male offspring to travel with them post-boot and often the mamas will force them to disperse from their natal territory. So I am almost certain that the these bears are a mama and her two female yearlings, a very rare sight at this time of year!

Apples for a Main Course – Black Bear Style

People love apples, right? Perhaps they are a favorite snack while out for a hike or a favorite pie? Well, fellow humans, we are not alone in our hankering for apples! Black Bears LOVE apples, too!

One of my favorite sightings of apple-feasting bears occurred one June day several years ago. A mama bear and her two cubs were frequenting one forested area and I spent about six hours watching them forage on ground vegetation. They only moved about .25 mile in six hours! The next day I returned to the same area to look for them and I found them again, about a half mile from where I had seen them the previous day.

About an hour after I started watching them forage, they climbed up an apple tree. Short and rounded apple trees are easy to recognize, but I was puzzled why mama bear was taking her cubs up an apple tree in the middle of June, as apples don't ripen until July.

Once they got up in the tree and started eating, I suspected they were eating the leaves of the apple tree. But then I realized that they were actually eating *apples* — the very small, completely unripe, sour green apples! I was shocked!

Since then I have witnessed bears eating completely unripe apples in the month of June on a few other occasions. This is just one of many things I see each year that reminds me that the phrase "A bear will eat anything but rock!" is nearly true. For a Black Bear, unripe green apples (and unripe green acorns) = Yum!

An Evening in the Cherry Grove

One August evening my bear watching friend and I found a mama bear and two cubs that we know well in the heart of their territory. They share this territory with a different mama bear that was raising three cubs that year. The mama and two cubs were walking through the forest, slowly meandering their way towards the top of a hill. We hiked a trail to the top of the hill, just a couple minutes walk, in hopes of meeting up with the trio as they ascended. The next part of the story may seem confusing as I was certainly confused once I got to the top of the hill!

When we got up there we spotted a mama bear and her cubs up in a cherry tree eating wild Black Cherries. We were surprised that the family had made it up to the top of the tree so quickly and without our hearing them climb up. Then we realized that there were four bears in the tree, a mama and her three cubs! Had we misidentified the original family?

Perhaps the family that we had seen originally at the bottom of the hill was the mama and three cubs that were now in the tree and not the mama and two like we thought? Perhaps we somehow didn't see the third cub when the family was on the ground? Soon all the pieces of the puzzle came together. We spotted *more bears* walking on the ground, just yards away from the tree that the mama and three cubs were in. It was the mama and two that we had originally seen at the base of the hill! It was quite an awesome experience to be in the presence of seven bears, two mamas and their five cubs total, all in one small grove of cherry trees.

Bears are usually solitary, except when mamas are with their cubs and during mating season. It is certainly fairly unusual to see two families in close proximity. I believe that these two mothers are related to each other, perhaps as sisters, and that this may well explain why they tolerated each other as much as they did.

The mom and two cubs soon went on their way. My friend and I stayed and observed the mama and three as they ate cherries up in the tree. We stayed with them for an hour at which point the family climbed out of the tree and I got my favorite photo of the evening, of one of the three cubs silhouetted against the darkening sky at dusk.

The Art of Tree Feasting

This is an adult female bear that I know well up in a cherry tree. It might be hard to understand at first, but believe me, she is about 60 feet up in a very tall, wild Black Cherry tree!

Black Bears are very smart animals, and they will use their body parts as tools as much as they possibly can. What this bear did right before I took this photo is a great example of this! Do you see the snapped branch off to her right in this photograph? About 30 seconds before I took this photo it was standing straight and tall, like any normal branch. It held a large collection of yummy cherries that Ms. Bear wanted to eat, but the branch was a little too thin to support her body weight.

So she gnawed the branch with her teeth until it snapped, and then she was able to simply pull the branch to her with her paws so that she could feast on all the cherries! Amazingly enough, this is a not at all uncommon tactic for bears to use while they are feasting in trees. I see it many times each year with apple, cherry, oak, and hickory tree-feasting bears.

I love watching bears gorge on cherries and it is a truly exciting thing for any avid bear watcher to experience. One of the many reasons for our amazement is just how cool it is to get to watch bears in trees displaying behavior showing off their intelligence, such as branch-breaking to reach otherwise inaccessible food.

Did you know? Bears are the most intelligent non-human land mammals in North America. No wonder they know how to get to out-of-reach foods in trees, with ease!

Drive the Speed Limit!

One early Autumn day my dad and I found this large adult male bear crossing the road while chasing a younger bear out of an oak grove that he wanted all to himself. Dominant males like this big fellow are known for defending their food sources when subordinate bears enter their feeding area. Moments before I took this photo the subordinate bear crossed the road, and this big guy was focused on chasing him out of his feeding area while not paying attention to the road at all.

Black Bears cross roadways frequently, day and night. Sometimes bears will pause and wait to make sure that the coast is clear before crossing. Other times they will cross suddenly — especially cubs trying to catch up to their mom or a male in mating season trying to keep up with a female bear. In these situations bears will simply walk or run into the road without warning, causing a potentially dangerous situation.

In Black Bear country, as much as anywhere, speed limits are important to obey. Even if it appears that no wildlife are around, *they are there!* You just may not see them. But one thing is for sure: if you *do* see wildlife you want to see them in a natural, happy, healthy way, not under your tires or damaging your car! It is *always* important when in Black Bear habitat or in habitat of any other wild animal to remember that you are in their home, not ours. Driving the speed limit greatly decreases the chance of a life-ending encounter for a bear or other animal and is the easiest and most important way to respect animals when in their home.

A September to Remember

Autumn is a season of "feast or famine" both for bears and bear lovers like myself. From September through early December, when most Black Bears enter their winter dens, 80% of bears' food source comes from nuts, especially acorns and hickory nuts. Several species of oak and several species of hickory produce nuts each fall. Some crops are plentiful, others are insufficient. Even if most of the species of oak and hickory produce insufficient crops in a given autumn, bears can still get enough food to survive winter if just a couple of species of nut-producing trees yield massive crops.

White oak is one of the species of nut-producing trees that first offers nuts in the fall. One September the White Oak acorn crop was unique and one that I will never forget. Most of the White Oaks in a certain large area of Blue Ridge woodlands produced a below average crop of acorns, but one area with a large population of White Oaks produced enough acorns to feed over a dozen bears for a month!

As the White Oak acorns were abundant in just this one area, bears from surrounding territories concentrated in this one oak grove, coming and going throughout day and night. The area was large enough that they rarely had to feast close to one another, and they never got into conflicts. For bear observers like myself, it was heaven on earth. Each different corner of the oak grove held a bear or a family of bears. They spent most of their time up in trees but also spent a considerable amount of time on the ground, eating nuts that had fallen when they shook and broke branches while eating.

My biggest hope each fall is that my bear friends have a large enough food supply to sustain them through fall and winter. However, when I get my wish and the nut crop is plentiful, I rarely see my bear friends because they don't have to move around much and become isolated from both other bears and humans. They, simply put, eat the fall away out of my view!

On the flip side, during years when nut crops fail, emaciated bears become a common sight, roaming far and wide for any food they can find. I may see more bears in years like that than when the nut crop is plentiful, but it breaks my heart to see sickly bears and I'd rather see no bears at all and know that they are getting their needed nourishment. This one particular year I got the best of both worlds. I got to see a lot of bears in an area where there was a huge supply of food, and every bear was healthy and happy. I will never forget that amazing September and hope to have another one like it!

Did you know? Each fall from September through early December Black Bears undergo a phase called "hyperphagia" where they eat 20 hours a day to fatten up for winter! They can consume 20,000 calories per day, and subadults and females nearly double their summer weight in three months!

Hurt Mama

The encounter during which I took these photographs is still one of my most amazing, memorable, and unique bear encounters to date.

It took place on an October afternoon in an area of the Appalachian Mountains that had a high population of bears and which is one of my favorite spots to watch bears.

One family living in that area was a specific mama bear and her 2 cubs that I had the honor of spending a lot of time with. I watched them day in and day out as they were easily visible eating from a specific oak grove. I definitely developed a very tender spot in my heart for this wonderful family.

Then one day my mom and I were hiking along one of the trails through that oak grove and way up ahead we heard some loud vocalizations. I thought they were fellow hikers with a crying baby in the distance but my mom was convinced we were hearing a bear cub. In this case, my mom was right! We hiked about 50 more yards and off the trail to our right we saw the mama and one of her two cubs. It was my most bittersweet bear moment up to that point in my life. The sweetness was that we were watching a mama and a cub 50 yards off the trail — the bitterness was that it was very apparent that the mama was quite hurt.

The cub at her side was crying loudly, "WAAH!" "WAAH!" every 20 seconds or so. The mama was obviously in a lot of pain as she just lay there, not moving a bit, with her head on the ground. Obviously the cub was very concerned about his mama and kept crying. At one point the hurt mama got so annoyed with her cub crying that she swatted him off to her side!

What is so interesting about this encounter is that while mama was so injured, with one cub so scared right at her side, the second cub was about 75 yards away feeding on downed acorns without an apparent worry or care in the world! This is an amazingly clear example of the difference between a "butt-baby" (a cub that never wants to leave mama's side) and an "adventuresome cub" (a cub that will try and get away with anything: exploring, lingering behind, digging in places it shouldn't, etc, regardless of mama's instructions).

I wondered what had happened to my mama bear friend. I wondered if she had fallen out of a tree or maybe been a hit by a car. But the latter seemed unlikely as she was so immobile and we were at least a quarter mile from the road. We left to alert rangers about the bears and then returned to check on them. We watched them for a long while and she only moved about three feet in three hours! I was so discouraged when we headed home that evening and I hoped that mama bear would make it through this big challenge.

Five days later we returned to the oak grove and received the best news possible! Half a mile from where we had experienced the bittersweet hours five days before, we found our bear family friends. Mama was up and walking, almost normally. She was hobbling a little, but not much! We were so happy. It was truly awesome to be able to witness this amazing cycle from health to injury and back to health again!

If you ever hit a bear or find an injured bear please report it to a ranger, police officer or wildlife official as soon as possible, either in person or by phone!

Keep Track of Your Cubs, or Else!

One late November day my friend and I were on a ridge where we had frequently been seeing a particular mama bear and her three cubs. We were hoping to find them again before they entered their winter den.

Well our wish was more than fulfilled! As we reached the top of the ridge, we spotted several bears very near each other. There were at least four bears, and most of them were small. We believed that we were looking at the mama bear and three cubs that we were looking for. And for a minute that made sense! Then we noticed that there were definitely more than four bears! There were five, then six, and at one point both of us thought we saw seven bears all in this one small area!

It turns out that we *did* see S-E-V-E-N bears! It was the mama and three cubs *and* a second mama and two cubs that also live in that area. I believe that the two mamas are related to one other. When we first spotted them the two families were very close to each other but soon separated and began feeding about 60 yards apart.

As I like to say, "There is always a kid in every crowd" and I would say that is often true for bears, too! One cub will just refuse to listen to mama and wander off on his or her own. That is exactly what one of the cubs from the two-cub litter did this particular day. He left his mama and walked over to the mama and three cubs, curiously checking out what the mama and three were doing.

Once the mama of three noticed the little invader, she wanted NONE OF IT! She ran over to the cub, which proceeded to jump up onto the side of a tree. Then the mama of the three circled the base of the tree on her hind legs, huffing and popping her jaws in signs of aggression at the "invading" cub! She even took a swat at the cub! After about twenty seconds of circling, jaw popping, and a swat, the mama of the three finally backed off and retreated to her own cubs. The scared-for-his-life little cub then jumped off the tree and sprinted over to reunite with his mama and sibling.

Well about ten minutes later one of the three cubs from the larger family got the same idea as the rascal from the first litter and started walking over towards where the mama and two cubs were feeding. That mama also wanted nothing to do with an invader from a different litter! She ran over to the cub, which also jumped on a tree. The mama of the two circled that tree like the mama from the other litter had done just ten minutes earlier! This younger mama was not as aggressive, and only circled the base of the tree on all fours and did not jaw pop or swat. Eventually she returned to her cubs as well and the scared adventurous cub from the three cub litter ran back and reunited with his mama and two siblings. Once the little cub reunited with its mama, the two of them shared a brief play session that I captured in the photo below, and mama reassured her cub that everything was okay again!

It was an encounter with bears unlike anything I had ever experienced. The food was getting scarce in the forest and I believe the mamas were aggressive towards the "invading cubs" due to the fact that they wanted to keep as many of the nuts as possible for themselves and their own cubs!

Life Can Be Hard

Here are two cubs that I spent a lot of time with one November. Two families of bears (a mama and two cubs and a mama and three cubs) and several single bears were attracted to an oak grove containing one of fall's last nut supplies.

The area in which these bears reside has a very dense bear population, so most of the trees' nut supplies had been exhausted, but bears had not yet hit this one oak grove. It had one of the last good supplies of food of the whole year. It was a wonderful experience for my mom and me to spend so much time with these new bear friends.

These two youngsters were quite interesting cubs to observe. We were camping nearby and for 48 hours we spent time off-and-on with these bears. For the first 36 hours the cubs were acting as typical, wonderful, adventuresome cubs feasting on acorns while their mama also feasted nearby!

On the morning of the third day, we noticed one of the cubs was acting differently. The darker-snouted one (on the left in this photograph) was now walking on only three legs and dragging the fourth one along, and it had a large section of the back of its rear right leg torn off.

We wondered what had happened, but soon noticed that a huge adult male bear had moved into the area overnight — and males are known to occasionally go after cubs. After all, there were only a certain number of

nuts in the oak grove, and the male wanted them for himself. And certainly some little cub wasn't going to get his nuts, if he had anything to say about it!

That afternoon my mom and I had to head home from our camping trip and we wished our bear friends well, especially the little guy walking on three legs. We returned to that oak grove over the coming days and weeks and found several other bears, but we couldn't re-find the mama and two cubs.

I have not been able to find this little guy or his sibling again, and unfortunately have little hope that he remains alive. That attack by the male was probably fatal, and he likely died over that winter. It is always sad when I lose one of my bear friends but he was a special little bear who taught me how hard it can be to be young in the wild, that's for darn sure.

Hickory Ridge

Here are two shots of different bears that I had the honor of getting to spend a lot of time with one November.

That particular fall a lot of bears — including some subadults, a couple of mamas with cubs, and a large male — converged on a ridge in the forest for one reason: the nut crop. While elsewhere the nut crop had been slightly below average, this one particular ridge produced a downright massive crop of hickory nuts and all area bears were there to take full advantage of it!

It was a fantastic experience to get to watch these bears of all different sizes, shapes, and ages, feasting on this bountiful food supply of late fall.

I remember one time spending about two hours watching the left hand bear above foraging on the ground eating hickory nuts that had fallen out of the trees. Then I walked a little farther along the ridge and came across a mama bear and two cubs, and I watched them for a couple more hours as they ate nuts in a hickory tree. Through my years of bear watching I've had several experiences like this where I have opportunities to spend a lot of time watching "congregations" of bears at sites with high nut productivity. Each experience is unique — and this particular one I will always refer to fondly as "Hickory Ridge."

Grapes for Dessert

Through the year from April to early December, Black Bears eat a wide variety of foods that include young leaves, flowers, apples, cherries, berries, ant larvae, some meat and lots and lots of nuts during the fall.

There's one last wonderful treat that the bears get to enjoy before they enter their winter dens. In late November, just days or weeks before they den, Wild grapes ripen in small numbers in the quieting woods. There aren't enough grapes to truly sustain bears but they are a welcome break from a diet of nuts and provide some important additional nutrition right before they enter their dens. I like to call it a "special dessert" for Black Bears at the end of their year of eating!

For several years I had heard stories of bears eating wild grapes but it took me quite a while to actually luck into finding a bear in some grape vines. Then one particular fall I was fortunate enough to see this occur several times. There was a very good grape crop that year and it was a great opportunity to study bears at the very end of autumn enjoying this last sweet treat before entering their winter dens.

The Forest Goes To Sleep

Each year the beginning of December is a bittersweet time for me because my year with the bears is coming to an end. By the middle of December, bears have consumed most of the nuts and other food out in the forest and it is time for the bears to head into their winter dens.

Bears spend most of the winter in their dens, and they do not eat, drink, urinate, or defecate for several months! If there is an unusually warm winter day it may get hot in the den and they may emerge and just lounge around, sleeping the day away at the entrance of their den, before crawling back in once it cools down at night.

Black Bears in the eastern mountains do not truly hibernate. Their heart rate does not slow down quite enough to be considered true hibernation. "Winter denning period," "winter lethargy," or "semi-hibernation" are better terms for our beloved eastern Black Bears' long winter nap. (True hibernating bears, like Grizzlies and Western Black Bears, sleep completely through the winter and do not come out of their dens at all.)

All winter long I miss my bear friends terribly, but winter is a very special time for them. Even though I don't see them for four months or so, I feel close to them. I think of the mamas giving birth to their

new cubs in mid-winter and I think of the young ones that I have spent so much time with over the past year as they turn one year old.

Through the winter I anticipate with excitement the coming spring and the rebirth of the forest. The barren bear-less woods of winter will become green again with little cubs running around exploring their home for the first time.

Simply put, even though it seems like the bears disappear, winter is really a time of rebirth for the Black Bear community and even though I do not see my bear friends for months I carry their spirit with me during a crucial time of year for them.

As you may imagine, I do not have many winter bear photos but I would like to share with you a couple of favorites taken during the late autumn of healthy bears preparing to enter their winter dens.

I hope you've enjoyed sharing a year in the life of Black Bears with me!

Black Bear Facts

Female Black Bears are called "sows," males are called "boars," and babies are called "cubs."

Black Bear cubs are born in their mothers' winter dens in January and February. They weigh 8-12 ounces at birth and are furless with their eyes closed. They emerge in late April weighing 4-8 pounds, at which time they are furry and have their eyes open.

Black Bear cubs generally remain with their mother for 16 months. She sets them out on their own in late May-early June of their second year so that she can mate again and prepare to raise her next litter. (Female Black Bears have cubs every other year).

Adult male Black Bears are larger than females and are sometimes more than double the size. Adult female eastern Black Bears generally weigh 125-300 pounds. Adult males generally weigh 250-400 pounds with some even topping 600 pounds.

80% of an Eastern Black Bear's diet is vegetarian. The remaining 20% of their diet consists of larvae, roadkill, winter-die-off mammals and White-tailed Deer fawns in the spring.

Black Bears are active at all times of day and night, but especially during the hot summer months they prefer to be active closer to dawn and dusk. Animals active at dawn and dusk are called "crepuscular."

Eastern Black Bears do not truly hibernate. Their heart rates do not slow down as much as those of true hibernating animals. They are also more active in the wintertime than true hibernating mammals if it gets warm or if food becomes available. "Winter lethargy," "semi-hibernation," and "winter denning period" are more accurate terms.

Black Bear Resources

Here are a few organizations that do amazing work to help Black Bears and to help people understand them.

The North American Bear Center: bear.org

Bear With Us: bearwithus.org

Get Bear Smart Society: bearsmart.com

Appalachian Bear Rescue: appalachianbearrescue.org

and your local state park, national forest, national park, or other natural area where Black Bears live!

Praise for Gabriel's First Book: "Oh No, Gertrude!"

"An insightful, accurate book — everyone young and old needs to hear the message Gabriel presents here: we have a people problem not a bear problem! The future of these present, intelligent, and misunderstood animals depends on it. Gabriel is an amazing boy who has a profound love of wild animals coupled with an innate understanding of bears — this type of understanding is a gift, one that few in this world have."

— Chris Day, Naturalist and co-star with the Bears
in the National Wildlife Federation film BEARS IMAX

"Oh No, Gertrude!"

The True Story of a Not-So-Naughty Black Bear
by Gabriel Mapel, age 10
photographs by Rodney Cammauf

"Oh No, Gertrude!" is a children's picture book that tells the true story of a mama bear and her three cubs whose lives were put into danger by naughty people who left unattended food out on picnic tables. The book is a delightful story, with a very happy ending, that educates young and old about what they can do to help keep Black Bears safe. "Oh No, Gertrude!" was published in 2010 in collaboration with wildlife photographer Rodney Cammauf. It has sold more than 7,500 copies in national parks around the USA.

Available at Gabriel's website: **wildwithgabriel.com**

CPSIA information can be obtained at www.ICGtesting.com
Printed in the USA
BVIW12n2146071216
470135BV00013B/118